GERAR.

Poems selected by JOHN STAMMERS

Gerard Manley Hopkins (1844–1889) was born in Stratford (formerly in Essex). He attended Balliol College, Oxford where he befriended the future Poet Laureate, Robert Bridges. While at Balliol he converted to Roman Catholicism and after graduating he entered the Society of Jesus and was ordained in 1877. Having burned his early poems on entering the Church, Hopkins eventually took up writing again but apart from a few poems that appeared in periodicals he was not published during his own lifetime. Since the publication of his poems in 1918 he has become one of the best-known poets of the Victorian age and his are among the greatest poems written on the subject of faith and doubt.

John Stammers read philosophy at King's College London and is an Associate of King's College. His first collection, *Panoramic Lounge-bar* (2001), was awarded the Forward Prize for Best First Collection and shortlisted for the Whitbread Poetry Award; his second, *Stolen Love Behaviour* (2005), was a Poetry Book Society Choice. A creative writing tutor and freelance writer, he lives in Hampstead, London, with his wife and their two sons. *Interior Night* was published by Picador in 2010.

GERARD MANLEY HOPKINS

Poems selected by JOHN STAMMERS

faber and faber

First published in 2012
by Faber and Faber Limited
Bloomsbury House, 74–77 Great Russell Street
London WC1B 3DA

Typeset by RefineCatch Limited, Bungay, Suffolk
Printed in England by CPI Group (UK) Ltd, Croydon CR0 4YY

A CIP record for this book
is available from the British Library

ISBN 978–0–571–23068–6

10 9 8 7 6 5 4 3 2 1

Contents

Introduction

In an art form that is thought to value originality, it is a puzzle that, in the history of poetry, few truly original poets have emerged. When one thinks of those generally reckoned as originals one comes up with perhaps: Herbert, Coleridge, Blake, or Dickinson, then later E. E. Cummings, Dylan Thomas, John Berryman; and today we might pick out Les Murray and Paul Muldoon. Despite the being thought of as originals, however, these poets do seem to have features in common. They share an unusually highly developed experiential imagination that ranges from the oxymoronic through magical, surreal and dreamscape all the way to the downright psychedelic. Also they exhibit a virtuosity with form and sound, often leading to a concentration on lexical form. To the above names we must add Gerard Manley Hopkins (1844–89), widely judged pre-eminently to merit the term *sui generis*, one of a kind. 'Every poet,' wrote Hopkins, 'must be original and originality a condition of poetic genius; so that each poet is like a species in nature . . . and can never recur.'

Hopkins was born in 1844 in Stratford in what was then Essex, but is now part of the Greater London borough of Newham and the site of the 2012 Olympic Games. He attended Highgate School (a stone's throw, as it turns out, from Coleridge's last home, and his last resting place, St Michael's Church). Hopkins showed talent at Highgate and won the school poetry prize. Despite an early start, however, Hopkins's output was sparse: seventy-six poems plus another eighty or so fragments. Of these he lived to see only a handful in print. In this edition, I have selected all the most well-known of his poems, together with others that I thought to be significant or distinctive.

Hopkins's ability at school poetry may not be unrelated to the fact that, in common with Dylan Thomas's, Hopkins's father was himself a poet. Hopkins père had published a volume dedicated to Thomas Hood. Hopkins would certainly know, for instance:

Mad from life's history,
Glad to death's mystery,
Swift to be hurl'd –
Anywhere, anywhere,
Out of the world!
(Thomas Hood, 'The Bridge of Sighs', 1844)

Although Hopkins is not noted to have been directly influenced by Hood, it might still furnish us with one way of thinking about Hopkins himself. A particular sort of out-of-the-mundane-world attitude characterised his views and his verse. Highgate Village is perched high above North London. North London is where I too spent my childhood, being schooled lower down the hill at Holloway. I can report that, rare for London, there remains, even to this day, a distinct flavour of the country village about Highgate. In the middle of the nineteenth century this would have been yet the more so for the young Hopkins. Highgate sits atop a high hill directly to the north of the city. From this vantage point, Hopkins would have been able to observe first-hand the burgeoning of the metropolis of the empire.

As a student at Balliol College, Oxford, Hopkins joined the Roman Catholic Church. At Oxford, he also met the future Poet Laureate, Robert Bridges, who was to be a lifelong friend and one of the few people to read Hopkins's work when he was alive. It was Bridges who, after Hopkins's death, approached the Daniel Press with a view to publishing a selection of his verse. Without this intervention we would very likely be without Hopkins's work today. Two years after having taken a first in Greats, Hopkins commenced training as a Jesuit. This extra discipline, requiring the subject as it does to devote their mind fully to the service of Christ, led Hopkins to renounce his poetry and burn his earlier verses. Hopkins eventually found himself in North Wales where, characteristically, he set about learning Welsh. This would feed into his verse as the 'constant chime' he heard in the language. It was in North Wales, after the passage of seven years from his poetic renunciation, under the encouragement of his rector, that Hopkins wrote 'The Wreck of the Deutschland'. In that key poem he first put into effect the full range of his technical innovations. This was the start of his mature verse which comprises his most famous works.

By the end of his life, Hopkins would have lived in London, Oxford, Birmingham, Dublin, Liverpool, Glasgow and Chesterfield. For most of this time he was a serving priest. He developed 'a conviction, a truly crushing conviction, of the misery of town life to the poor and more than to the poor'. Of Liverpool, for example, he was to write, 'of all places the most museless'. The only completed poem it seems he wrote there was 'Felix Randal', which meditates on the life and fate of a working man rather than nature. On the other hand, he wrote the beautiful pastoral lyric 'Spring and Fall' at Rose Hill, Lydiate, some miles *outside* Liverpool. What can be detected throughout his poetry (e.g. 'The Windhover', 'Pied Beauty', 'Binsey Poplars') is that particular fascination for the pastoral that can be formed only by a hard familiarity with the urban.

Hopkins's contemplation of nature came to include an account of how natural objects – people, animals, the moon, nature in general, everything not man-made – were constituted. Hopkins believed natural objects consisted of a set of qualities unified uniquely in that thing. By natural object here is meant not, for instance, an apple in the sense of all apples in general, but a single apple, *this* apple I hold in my hand, as it were. It is its specific qualities of redness and shininess, and the precise shape of this apple that make it what it is. Hopkins developed these ideas into his theory of 'oneness'. Typically, there not being a term he was aware of at the time, he coined a word: *inscape*. An object's inscape is its constituent qualities and their particular configuration in it. The qualities he identifies are those available to human perceptual experience, generally what have been termed sense impressions. In this regard, Hopkins's conception is a form of empiricism not unlike that of David Hume. It is distinctive, however, in the fact that he thinks these sense impressions are the outer expression of the inner essence of that thing. So the blueness of a kingfisher or the brindle of a cow are manifestations of their inscape but also real constituents of it. Or consider 'daylight's dauphin, dapple-dawn-drawn Falcon, in his riding' ('The Windhover'). Here Hopkins is practically listing inscape qualities of that singular bird of prey. These special patterns are the blueprints and evidence of God's design and attention. 'And not one [sparrow] . . . falls to the ground apart from your Father's will. But the very hairs of your head are all numbered.' (Matthew 10: 29–31). This attention manifests as *instress*, which is the term Hopkins was forced to coin to account for the energy by which inscape was held in place. Instress is present everywhere there is inscape. The particular combination of inscape and instress in this apple makes it what it is.

There is a sense, of course, in which Hopkins's notion of the uniqueness of individual items is a truism. But for Hopkins there was a more important weight to it. Imagine if we were speaking about a person. It is, of course, trivial to say you are no one else but who you are. It is *not* trivial, though, to point out who you in fact are and in what distinct, distinctive and, hopefully, delightful ways. Indeed, Hopkins could be said to have fathered the hippyish notion that everything is beautiful in its own way. For Hopkins, any natural object is as distinct as a person, as if, for example, every leaf had a proper name. It is, after all, the Windhover who is called 'dauphin', prince, and note the word 'Falcon' is capitalised. For the definitive statement, consider the first stanza of 'As kingfishers catch fire . . .'

As kingfishers catch fire, dragonflies draw flame;
      As tumbled over rim in roundy wells
      Stones ring; like each tucked string tells, each hung bell's
Bow swung finds tongue to fling out broad its name;
Each mortal thing does one thing and the same:
      Deals out that being indoors each one dwells;
      Selves – goes itself; *myself* it speaks and spells,
Crying *Whát I do is me: for that I came.*

It might be thought unsurprising that Hopkins, being a priest, thought of natural objects as the direct handiwork of God. This idea is by no means straightforward, however, even to a believer. But I think it would have been inconceivable to Hopkins that anything natural could be beautiful and *not* due to God. In fact, he was so attuned to this attitude that he was able to see a new beauty in hitherto unconsidered places, dappled things, for instance: 'Landscape plotted and pieced – fold, fallow and plough' ('Pied Beauty').

Later Hopkins would be much buoyed by the writings of the Oxford philosopher and theologian Duns Scotus, 'the Subtle Doctor' (1266–1308). These provided an established theological corroboration of his theories (see his poem 'Duns Scotus's Oxford'). It is remarkable to think of how Hopkins would have thought of himself, when contemplating a bird or leaf, as casting his eyes over the very fingerprints of God. Never was it truer of anyone to say that it all depends on how you look at it. To paraphrase another poet, William Blake: if the doors of perception were cleansed everything would appear to man as it is: *inscape*! And is it not the case that, seen aright, an apple *is* a miracle? In the television age we have become used to seeing the miraculous up-close and personal. We are now familiar with the type of slow-motion, precision view of a kingfisher, say, that is commonplace on David Attenborough programmes. It is as if, however, Hopkins were capable of those sorts of perceptions with just his naked eye; or should I say *mind*.

It seems clear to me that Hopkins and some of his fellow poets mentioned above were able to open the doors of perception by pure force of imagination analogous in some ways to the action of hallucinogenic drugs. (In some cases, of course, they indeed did avail themselves of mind-altering drugs – think of Coleridge). Hopkins, though, possessed a natural heightened sensitivity to the world which amounted to a gift. Returning to the quotation from Hood, Hopkins's out-of-the-world sensibility is away from the dull, unremarked world of everyday perception to the genuine world, composed of, and redolent with, inscape. So, perhaps the recognition of the force of inscape has to do with it being experienced under the right conditions.

Hopkins certainly thought that one of these conditions was poetry. It was practically his *raison d'être* for his writing poems: 'what I am in the habit of calling *inscape* is what I above all aim at in poetry.' He says, '[poetry is] speech framed for contempla- tion of the mind by the way of hearing or speech framed to be heard for its own sake and interest even over and above the interest of meaning'. This must mean that, for Hopkins, inscape in poetry is predominantly a matter of sound together with what we might call *rhetorical force*. If this view is right, it goes to explain why Hopkins's verse is chock-full of sound effects, unu- sual rhythms and brand-new words. Hopkins developed sprung rhythm which, Hopkins informs his brother Everard, 'gives back to poetry its true soul and self.' These new rhythms, fresh yet natural, met Hopkins's desire to convey to the reader an experi- ence of the apprehension of inscape comparable to his own. In terms of imagery, he could not do this by, say, describing the embers of fire in a straightforward way. A normal person's expe- rience of them (in an age when 'real' fires were commonplace) would just be unremarkable. Hopkins perforce must conjure a wonderful confection of words, rhythm and passion to do the job. The embers of the fire: 'fall, gall themselves, gash gold- vermillion.' This fecund inscape is designed to be epiphanic.

As a form, the writing of poetry demands an ability to make use of the intellectual along with the intuitive, emotional or spiritual – the considered *and* the felt. It is sometimes thought that the writing of a poem is pure inspiration, and indeed inspi- ration of some sort is perhaps an instigating force. But it must be managed and directed, somewhat like riding a spirited horse: the rider has neither the power of the horse nor the outright capacity to control it, but the horse may be steered in the right direction, governed by the skill of the rider. In Hopkins we find a remarkable union of a thoroughly analytic intellectualism with a form of extreme mysticism. It is analysis, as this is the detailed intellectual exploration of how the world appeared; the mysticism being Hopkins's intuition that this was the *direct* manifestation of God's handiwork.

So, returning to those qualities those 'original' poets we named at the outset seem to have in common, it seems to me that in Hopkins the imaginative tendency is primary. He is struck by the inscape of the world. He then, as we have seen, needs to express this in verse. Given the nature of the task, he is drawn to employ dense forms and passionate rhetoric. This goes some way to account for, in his case, the emphasis on sound effects: rhythm, rhyme, alliteration, assonance, etc. To write his verse, however, Hopkins had to be able to make use of another talent. I want to mention one aspect of that. This is the fact that Hopkins was a master of the craft of what I will call, for the sake of simplicity, *structure*.

The poem of Hopkins's which for me exemplifies this most clearly is 'Felix Randal'. Written in that classic lyric form the Petrarchan sonnet, it is about a farrier who has succumbed to tuberculosis, or consumption as was. 'Some fatal four disorders, fleshed there, all contended', is Hopkins's horrific image of the disease's manifold assault. Hopkins's mastery of the lyric is exemplified by the encapsulating phrase in Felix Randal. Amid all the opulent long lines and multi-phrased, elliptical sentences of the rest of the poem one three-word sentence stands out: 'Sickness broke him.' This is the shocking conclusion about this most powerful of men: that disease and death are stronger than him. As we then see, he 'mended', due to the intervention of his priest Hopkins and the 'sweet reprieve and ransom' of faith. 'Sickness broke him' is the fixed point in the writhing, smelting mass of the piece. It is that from which everything else flows. It is Hopkins's anvil. It shows him as the master craftsman at poetry's grim forge as he fettles for us the bright and battering sandal of his verse.

JOHN STAMMERS

GERARD MANLEY HOPKINS

Spring and Fall
to a young child

Márgarét, áre you gríeving
Over Goldengrove unleaving?
Leáves, líke the things of man, you
With your fresh thoughts care for, can you?
Áh! ás the heart grows older
It will come to such sights colder
By and by, nor spare a sigh
Though worlds of wanwood leafmeal lie;
And yet you *will* weep and know why.
Now no matter, child, the name:
Sórrow's spríngs áre the same.
Nor mouth had, no nor mind, expressed
What heart heard of, ghost guessed:
It ís the blight man was born for,
It is Margaret you mourn for.

Hurrahing in Harvest

Summer ends now; now, barbarous in beauty, the stooks rise
Around; up above, what wind-walks! what lovely behaviour
Of silk-sack clouds! has wilder, wilful-wavier
Meal-drift moulded ever and melted across skies?

I walk, I lift up, I lift up heart, eyes,
Down all that glory in the heavens to glean our Saviour;
And, éyes, heárt, what looks, what lips yet gave you a
Rapturous love's greeting of realer, of rounder replies?

And the azurous hung hills are his world-wielding shoulder
Majestic – as a stallion stalwart, very-violet-sweet! –
These things, these things were here and but the beholder
Wanting; which two when they once meet,
The heart réars wíngs bold and bolder
And hurls for him, O half hurls earth for him off under
    his feet.

The May Magnificat

May is Mary's month, and I
Muse at that and wonder why:
     Her feasts follow reason,
     Dated due to season –

Candlemas, Lady Day;
But the Lady Month, May,
     Why fasten that upon her,
     With a feasting in her honour?

Is it only its being brighter
Than the most are must delight her?
     Is it opportunest
     And flowers finds soonest?

Ask of her, the mighty mother:
Her reply puts this other
     Question: What is Spring? –
     Growth in everything –

Flesh and fleece, fur and feather,
Grass and greenworld all together;
     Star-eyed strawberry-breasted
     Throstle above her nested

Cluster of bugle blue eggs thin
Forms and warms the life within;
     And bird and blossom swell
     In sod or sheath or shell.

All things rising, all things sizing
Mary sees, sympathising
     With that world of good,
     Nature's motherhood.

Their magnifying of each its kind
With delight calls to mind
      How she did in her stored
      Magnify the Lord.

Well but there was more than this:
Spring's universal bliss
      Much, had much to say
      To offering Mary May.

When drop-of-blood-and-foam-dapple
Bloom lights the orchard-apple
      And thicket and thorp are merry
      With silver-surfèd cherry

And azuring-over greybell makes
Wood banks and brakes wash wet like lakes
      And magic cuckoocall
      Caps, clears, and clinches all –

This ecstasy all through mothering earth
Tells Mary her mirth till Christ's birth
      To remember and exultation
      In God who was her salvation.

For a Picture of St Dorothea

I bear a basket lined with grass;
I am so light, I am so fair,
That men must wonder as I pass
And at the basket that I bear,
Where in a newly-drawn green litter
Sweet flowers I carry, – sweets for bitter.

Lilies I shew you, lilies none,
None in Caesar's gardens blow, –
And a quince in hand, – not one
Is set upon your boughs below;
Not set, because their buds not spring;
Spring not, 'cause world is wintering.

But these were found in the East and South
Where Winter is the clime forgot. –
The dewdrop on the larkspur's mouth
O should it then be quenchèd not?
In starry water-meads they drew
These drops: which be they? stars or dew?

Had she a quince in hand? Yet gaze:
Rather it is the sizing moon.
Lo, linkèd heavens with milky ways!
That was her larkspur row. – So soon?
Sphered so fast, sweet soul? – We see
Nor fruit, nor flowers, nor Dorothy.

As kingfishers catch fire, dragonflies draw flame;
  As tumbled over rim in roundy wells
  Stones ring; like each tucked string tells, each hung bell's
Bow swung finds tongue to fling out broad its name;
Each mortal thing does one thing and the same:
  Deals out that being indoors each one dwells;
  Selves – goes itself; *myself* it speaks and spells,
Crying *What I do is me: for that I came.*

Í say more: the just man justices;
  Keeps gráce: thát keeps all his goings graces;
Acts in God's eye what in God's eye he is –
  Chríst. For Christ plays in ten thousand places,
Lovely in limbs, and lovely in eyes not his
  To the Father through the features of men's faces.

The Loss of the Eurydice
Foundered March 24, 1878

The Eurydice – it concerned thee, O Lord:
Three hundred souls, O alas! on board,
    Some asleep unawakened, all un-
warned, eleven fathoms fallen

Where she foundered! One stroke
Felled and furled them, the hearts of oak!
    And flockbells off the aerial
Downs' forefalls beat to the burial.

For did she pride her, freighted fully, on
Bounden bales or a hoard of bullion? –
    Precious passing measure,
Lads and men her lade and treasure.

She had come from a cruise, training seamen –
Men, boldboys soon to be men:
    Must it, worst weather,
Blast bole and bloom together?

No Atlantic squall overwrought her
Or rearing billow of the Biscay water:
    Home was hard at hand
And the blow bore from land.

And you were a liar, O blue March day.
Bright sun lanced fire in the heavenly bay;
    But what black Boreas wrecked her? he
Came equipped, deadly-electric,

A beetling baldbright cloud thorough England
Riding: there did storms not mingle? and
    Hailropes hustle and grind their
Heavengravel? wolfsnow, worlds of it, wind there?

Now Carisbrook keep goes under in gloom;
Now it overvaults Appledurcombe;
    Now near by Ventnor town
It hurls, hurls off Boniface Down.

Too proud, too proud, what a press she bore!
Royal, and all her royals wore.
    Sharp with her, shorten sail!
Too late; lost; gone with the gale.

This was that fell capsize.
As half she had righted and hoped to rise
    Death teeming in by her portholes
Raced down decks, round messes of mortals.

Then a lurch forward, frigate and men;
'All hands for themselves' the cry ran then;
    But she who had housed them thither
Was around them, bound them or wound them with her.

Marcus Hare, high her captain,
Kept to her – care-drowned and wrapped in
    Cheer's death, would follow
His charge through the champ-white water-in-a-wallow,

All under Channel to bury in a beach her
Cheeks: Right, rude of feature,
    He thought he heard say
'Her commander! and thou too, and thou this way.'

It is even seen, time's something server,
In mankind's medley a duty-swerver,
    At downright 'No or Yes?'
Doffs all, drives full for righteousness.

Sydney Fletcher, Bristol-bred,
(Low lie his mates now on watery bed)
    Takes to the seas and snows
As sheer down the ship goes.

Now her afterdraught gullies him too down;
Now he wrings for breath with the deathgush brown;
    Till a lifebelt and God's will
Lend him a lift from the sea-swill.

Now he shoots short up to the round air;
Now he gasps, now he gazes everywhere;
    But his eye no cliff, no coast or
Mark makes in the rivelling snowstorm.

Him, after an hour of wintry waves,
A schooner sights, with another, and saves,
    And he boards her in Oh! such joy
He has lost count what came next, poor boy. –

They say who saw one sea-corpse cold
He was all of lovely manly mould,
    Every inch a tar,
Of the best we boast our sailors are.

Look, foot to forelock, how all things suit! he
Is strung by duty, is strained to beauty,
    And brown-as-dawning-skinned
With brine and shine and whirling wind.

O his nimble finger, his gnarled grip!
Leagues, leagues of seamanship
    Slumber in these forsaken
Bones, this sinew, and will not waken.

He was but one like thousands more.
Day and night I deplore
    My people and born own nation,
Fast foundering own generation.

I might let bygones be – our curse
Of ruinous shrine no hand or, worse,
    Robbery's hand is busy to
Dress, hoar-hallowèd shrines unvisited;

Only the breathing temple and fleet
Life, this wildworth blown so sweet,
        These daredeaths, ay this crew, in
Unchrist, all rolled in ruin –

Deeply surely I need to deplore it,
Wondering why my master bore it,
        The riving off that race
So at home, time was, to his truth and grace

That a starlight-wender of ours would say
The marvellous Milk was Walsingham Way
        And one – but let be, let be:
More, more than was will yet be. –

O well wept, mother have lost son;
Wept, wife; wept, sweetheart would be one:
        Though grief yield them no good
Yet shed what tears sad truelove should.

But to Christ lord of thunder
Crouch; lay knee by earth low under:
        'Holiest, loveliest, bravest,
Save my hero, O Hero savest.

And the prayer thou hearst me making
Have, at the awful overtaking,
        Heard; have heard and granted
Grace that day grace was wanted.'

Not that hell knows redeeming,
But for souls sunk in seeming
        Fresh, till doomfire burn all,
Prayer shall fetch pity eternal.

Duns Scotus's Oxford

Towery city and branchy between towers;
Cuckoo-echoing, bell-swarmèd, lark-charmèd, rook-racked,
  river-rounded;
The dapple-eared lily below thee; that country and town did
Once encounter in, here coped and poisèd powers;

Thou hast a base and brickish skirt there, sours
That neighbour-nature thy grey beauty is grounded
Best in; graceless growth, thou hast confounded
Rural rural keeping – folk, flocks, and flowers.

Yet ah! this air I gather and I release
He lived on; these weeds and waters, these walls are what
He haunted who of all men most sways my spirits to peace;

Of realty the rarest-veinèd unraveller; a not
Rivalled insight, be rival Italy or Greece;
Who fired France for Mary without spot.

Henry Purcell

The poet wishes well to the divine genius of Purcell and
praises him that, whereas other musicians have given
utterance to the moods of man's mind, he has, beyond that,
uttered in notes the very make and species of man as created
both in him and in all men generally.

Have fair fallen, O fair, fair have fallen, so dear
To me, so arch-especial a spirit as heaves in Henry Purcell,
An age is now since passed, since parted; with the reversal
Of the outward sentence low lays him, listed to a heresy, here.

Not mood in him nor meaning, proud fire or sacred fear,
Or love or pity or all that sweet notes not his might nursle:
It is the forgèd feature finds me; it is the rehearsal
Of own, of abrúpt sélf there so thrusts on, so throngs the ear.

Let him oh! with his air of angels then lift me, lay me! only I'll
Have an eye to the sakes of him, quaint moonmarks, to his
    pelted plumage under
Wings: so some great stormfowl, whenever he has walked his
    while

The thunder-purple seabeach plumèd purple-of-thunder,
If a wuthering of his palmy snow-pinions scatter a colossal
    smile
Off him, but meaning motion fans fresh our wits with
    wonder.

Felix Randal

Felix Randal the farrier, O is he dead then? my duty all ended,
Who have watched his mould of man, big-boned and hardy-
    handsome
Pining, pining, till time when reason rambled in it and some
Fatal four disorders, fleshed there, all contended?

Sickness broke him. Impatient, he cursed at first, but mended
Being anointed and all; though a heavenlier heart began some
Months earlier, since I had our sweet reprieve and ransom
Tendered to him. Ah well, God rest him all road ever he
    offended!
This seeing the sick endears them to us, us too it endears.
My tongue had taught thee comfort, touch had quenched thy
    tears,
Thy tears that touched my heart, child, Felix, poor Felix
    Randal;

How far from then forethought of, all thy more boisterous
    years,
When thou at the random grim forge, powerful amidst peers,
Didst fettle for the great grey drayhorse his bright and
    battering sandal!

The Handsome Heart
at a Gracious Answer

'But tell me, child, your choice; what shall I buy
You?' – 'Father, what you buy me I like best.'
With the sweetest air that said, still plied and pressed,
He swung to his first poised purport of reply.

What the heart is! which, like carriers let fly –
Doff darkness, homing nature knows the rest –
To its own fine function, wild and self-instressed,
Falls light as ten years long taught how to and why.

Mannerly-hearted! more than handsome face –
Beauty's bearing or muse of mounting vein,
All, in this case, bathed in high hallowing grace . . .

Of heaven what boon to buy you, boy, or gain
Not granted? – Only . . . O on that path you pace
Run all your race, O brace sterner that strain!

Heaven-Haven

A nun takes the veil

    I have desired to go
       Where springs not fail,
To fields where flies no sharp and sided hail
       And a few lilies blow.

    And I have asked to be
       Where no storms come,
Where the green swell is in the havens dumb,
       And out of the swing of the sea.

The Wreck of the Deutschland

*To the happy memory of five Franciscan nuns exiles by the Falck
Laws drowned between midnight and morning of Dec. 7th, 1875*

PART THE FIRST

1

Thou mastering me
God! giver of breath and bread;
World's strand, sway of the sea;
Lord of living and dead;
Thou hast bound bones and veins in me, fastened me flesh,
And after it almost unmade, what with dread,
Thy doing: and dost thou touch me afresh?
Over again I feel thy finger and find thee.

2

I did say yes
O at lightning and lashed rod;
Thou heardst me truer than tongue confess
Thy terror, O Christ, O God;
Thou knowest the walls, altar and hour and night:
The swoon of a heart that the sweep and the hurl of thee trod
Hard down with a horror of height:
And the midriff astrain with leaning of, laced with fire of stress.

3

The frown of his face
Before me, the hurtle of hell
Behind, where, where was a, where was a place?
I whirled out wings that spell
And fled with a fling of the heart to the heart of the Host.
My heart, but you were dovewinged, I can tell,
Carrier-witted, I am bold to boast,
To flash from the flame to the flame then, tower from the grace
to the grace.

4

I am soft sift

In an hourglass – at the wall

Fast, but mined with a motion, a drift,

And it crowds and it combs to the fall;

I steady as a water in a well, to a poise, to a pane,

But roped with, always, all the way down from the tall

Fells or flanks of the voel, a vein

Of the gospel proffer, a pressure, a principle, Christ's gift.

5

I kiss my hand

To the stars, lovely-asunder

Starlight, wafting him out of it; and

Glow, glory in thunder;

Kiss my hand to the dappled-with-damson west:

Since, tho' he is under the world's splendour and wonder,

His mystery must be instressed, stressed;

For I greet him the days I meet him, and bless when I understand.

6

Not out of his bliss

Springs the stress felt

Nor first from heaven (and few know this)

Swings the stroke dealt –

Stroke and a stress that stars and storms deliver,

That guilt is hushed by, hearts are flushed by and melt –

But it rides time like riding a river

(And here the faithful waver, the faithless fable and miss).

7

It dates from day

Of his going in Galilee;

Warm-laid grave of a womb-life grey;

Manger, maiden's knee;

The dense and the driven Passion, and frightful sweat:
Thence the discharge of it, there its swelling to be,
     Though felt before, though in high flood yet –
What none would have known of it, only the heart, being
  hard at bay,

8

               Is out with it! Oh,
          We lash with the best or worst
     Word last! How a lush-kept plush-capped sloe
          Will, mouthed to flesh-burst,
  Gush! – flush the man, the being with it, sour or sweet,
  Brim, in a flash, full! – Hither then, last or first,
          To hero of Calvary, Christ,'s feet –
Never ask if meaning it, wanting it, warned of it – men go.

9

               Be adored among men,
          God, three-numberèd form;
     Wring thy rebel, dogged in den,
          Man's malice, with wrecking and storm.
  Beyond saying sweet, past telling of tongue,
     Thou art lightning and love, I found it, a winter and warm;
          Father and fondler of heart thou hast wrung:
Hast thy dark descending and most art merciful then.

10

               With an anvil-ding
          And with fire in him forge thy will
     Or rather, rather then, stealing as Spring
          Through him, melt him but master him still:
  Whether at once, as once at a crash Paul,
  Or as Austin, a lingering-out swéet skíll,
          Make mercy in all of us, out of us all
Mastery, but be adored, but be adored King.

11

        'Some find me a sword; some
         The flange and the rail; flame,
   Fang, or flood' goes Death on drum,
        And storms bugle his fame.
  But wé dream we are rooted in earth – Dust!
 Flesh falls within sight of us, we, though our flower the same,
     Wave with the meadow, forget that there must
The sour scythe cringe, and the blear share come.

12

        On Saturday sailed from Bremen,
         American-outward-bound,
   Take settler and seamen, tell men with women,
        Two hundred souls in the round –
  O Father, not under thy feathers nor ever as guessing
  The goal was a shoal, of a fourth the doom to be drowned;
     Yet did the dark side of the bay of thy blessing
Not vault them, the million of rounds of thy mercy not reeve
  even them in?

13

        Into the snows she sweeps,
         Hurling the haven behind,
   The Deutschland, on Sunday; and so the sky keeps,
        For the infinite air is unkind,
  And the sea flint-flake, black-backed in the regular blow,
  Sitting Eastnortheast, in cursed quarter, the wind;
     Wiry and white-fiery and whirlwind-swivellèd snow
Spins to the widow-making unchilding unfathering deeps.

14

    She drove in the dark to leeward,
    She struck – not a reef or a rock
   But the combs of a smother of sand: night drew her
    Dead to the Kentish Knock;
 And she beat the bank down with her bows and the ride
  of her keel;
  The breakers rolled on her beam with ruinous shock;
    And canvas and compass, the whorl and the wheel
Idle for ever to waft her or wind her with, these she
  endured.

15

    Hope had grown grey hairs,
    Hope had mourning on,
   Trenched with tears, carved with cares,
    Hope was twelve hours gone;
 And frightful a nightfall folded rueful a day
  Nor rescue, only rocket and lightship, shone,
    And lives at last were washing away:
To the shrouds they took, – they shook in the hurling and
  horrible airs.

16

    One stirred from the rigging to save
    The wild woman-kind below,
   With a rope's end round the man, handy and brave –
    He was pitched to his death at a blow,
 For all his dreadnought breast and braids of thew:
  They could tell him for hours, dandled the to and fro
    Through the cobbled foam-fleece. What could he do
With the burl of the fountains of air, buck and the flood of
  the wave?

17

They fought with God's cold –
And they could not and fell to the deck
(Crushed them) or water (and drowned them) or rolled
With the sea-romp over the wreck.
Night roared, with the heart-break hearing a heart-broke
rabble,
The woman's wailing, the crying of child without check –
Till a lioness arose breasting the babble,
A prophetess towered in the tumult, a virginal tongue told.

18

Ah, touched in your bower of bone,
Are you! turned for an exquisite smart,
Have you! make words break from me here all alone,
Do you! – mother of being in me, heart.
O unteachably after evil, but uttering truth,
Why, tears! is it? tears; such a melting, a madrigal start!
Never-eldering revel and river of youth,
What can it be, this glee? the good you have there of your own?

19

Sister, a sister calling
A master, her master and mine! –
And the inboard seas run swirling and hawling;
The rash smart sloggering brine
Blinds her; but she that weather sees one thing, one;
Has one fetch in her: she rears herself to divine
Ears, and the call of the tall nun
To the men in the tops and the tackle rode over the storm's
brawling.

She was first of a five and came
Of a coifèd sisterhood.
(O Deutschland, double a desperate name!
O world wide of its good!
But Gertrude, lily, and Luther, are two of a town,
Christ's lily and beast of the waste wood:
From life's dawn it is drawn down,
Abel is Cain's brother and breasts they have sucked the same.)

21

Loathed for a love men knew in them,
Banned by the land of their birth,
Rhine refused them, Thames would ruin them;
Surf, snow, river and earth
Gnashed: but thou art above, thou Orion of light;
Thy unchancelling poising palms were weighing the worth,
Thou martyr-master: in thy sight
Storm flakes were scroll-leaved flowers, lily showers – sweet
heaven was astrew in them.

22

Five! the finding and sake
And cipher of suffering Christ.
Mark, the mark is of man's make
And the word of it Sacrificed.
But he scores it in scarlet himself on his own bespoken,
Before-time-taken, dearest prizèd and priced –
Stigma, signal, cinquefoil token
For lettering of the lamb's fleece, ruddying of the rose-flake.

23

        Joy fall to thee, father Francis,
        Drawn to the Life that died;
     With the gnarls of the nails in thee, niche of the lance, his
        Lovescape crucified
   And seal of his seraph-arrival! and these thy daughters
   And five-livèd and leavèd favour and pride,
      Are sisterly sealed in wild waters,
To bathe in his fall-gold mercies, to breathe in his all-fire glances.

24

        Away in the loveable west,
        On a pastoral forehead of Wales,
     I was under a roof here, I was at rest,
        And they the prey of the gales;
   She to the black-about air, to the breaker, the thickly
   Falling flakes, to the throng that catches and quails
      Was calling 'O Christ, Christ, come quickly':
The cross to her she calls Christ to her, christens her wild-worst
   Best.

25

        The majesty! what did she mean?
        Breathe, arch and original Breath.
     Is it love in her of the being as her lover had been?
        Breathe, body of lovely Death.
   They were else-minded then, altogether, the men
   Woke thee with a *We are perishing* in the weather of
     Gennesareth.
      Or is it that she cried for the crown then,
The keener to come at the comfort for feeling the combating
   keen?

        For how to the heart's cheering
        The down-dugged ground-hugged grey
     Hovers off, the jay-blue heavens appearing
        Of pied and peeled May!
  Blue-beating and hoary-glow height; or night, still higher,
  With belled fire and the moth-soft Milky Way,
     What by your measure is the heaven of desire,
The treasure never eyesight got, nor was ever guessed what for
  the hearing?

27

        No, but it was not these.
        The jading and jar of the cart,
     Time's tasking, it is fathers that asking for ease
        Of the sodden-with-its-sorrowing heart,
  Not danger, electrical horror; then further it finds
  The appealing of the Passion is tenderer in prayer apart:
     Other, I gather, in measure her mind's
Burden, in wind's burly and beat of endragonèd seas.

28

        But how shall I . . . make me room there:
        Reach me a . . . Fancy, come faster –
     Strike you the sight of it? look at it loom there,
        Thing that she . . . There then! the Master,
  Ipse, the only one, Christ, King, Head:
  He was to cure the extremity where he had cast her;
     Do, deal, lord it with living and dead;
Let him ride, her pride, in his triumph, despatch and have
  done with his doom there.

29

Ah! there was a heart right!
There was single eye!
Read the unshapeable shock night
And knew the who and the why;
Wording it how but by him that present and past,
Heaven and earth are word of, worded by? –
The Simon Peter of a soul! to the blast
Tarpeïan-fast, but a blown beacon of light.

30

Jesu, heart's light,
Jesu, maid's son,
What was the feast followed the night
Thou hadst glory of this nun? –
Feast of the one woman without stain.
For so conceivèd, so to conceive thee is done;
But here was heart-throe, birth of a brain,
Word, that heard and kept thee and uttered thee outright.

31

Well, she has thee for the pain, for the
Patience; but pity of the rest of them!
Heart, go and bleed at a bitterer vein for the
Comfortless unconfessed of them –
No not uncomforted: lovely-felicitous Providence
Finger of a tender of, O of a feathery delicacy, the breast of the
Maiden could obey so, be a bell to, ring of it, and
Startle the poor sheep back! is the shipwrack then a harvest, does
tempest carry the grain for thee?

32

        I admire thee, master of the tides,
          Of the Yore-flood, of the year's fall;
     The recurb and the recovery of the gulf's sides,
       The girth of it and the wharf of it and the wall;
   Stanching, quenching ocean of a motionable mind;
   Ground of being, and granite of it: past all
       Grasp God, throned behind
Death with a sovereignty that heeds but hides, bodes but abides;

33

        With a mercy that outrides
         The all of water, an ark
     For the listener; for the lingerer with a love glides
      Lower than death and the dark;
   A vein for the visiting of the past-prayer, pent in prison,
   The-last-breath penitent spirits – the uttermost mark
      Our passion-plungèd giant risen,
The Christ of the Father compassionate, fetched in the storm of
   his strides.

34

        Now burn, new born to the world,
         Double-naturèd name,
     The heaven-flung, heart-fleshed, maiden-furled
      Miracle-in-Mary-of-flame,
   Mid-numberèd he in three of the thunder-throne!
   Not a dooms-day dazzle in his coming nor dark as he came;
      Kind, but royally reclaiming his own;
A released shower, let flash to the shire, not a lightning of fire
   hard-hurled.

Dame, at our door
Drowned, and among our shoals,
Remember us in the roads, the heaven-haven of the reward:
Our King back, Oh, upon English souls!
Let him easter in us, be a dayspring to the dimness of us, be a
crimson-cresseted east,
More brightening her, rare-dear Britain, as his reign rolls,
Pride, rose, prince, hero of us, high-priest,
Our hearts' charity's hearth's fire, our thoughts' chivalry's throng's
Lord.

To what serves Mortal Beauty?

To what serves mortal beauty [|] – dangerous; does set danc-
ing blood – the O-seal-that-so [|] feature, flung prouder form
Than Purcell tune lets tread to? [|] See: it does this: keeps warm
Men's wits to the things that are; [|] what good means – where a
    glance
Master more may than gaze, [|] gaze out of countenance.
Those lovely lads once, wet-fresh [|] windfalls of war's storm,
How then should Gregory, a father, [|] have gleanèd else from
    swarm-
èd Rome? But God to a nation [|] dealt that day's dear chance.
To man, that needs would worship [|] block or barren stone,
Our law says: Love what are [|] love's worthiest, were all known;
World's loveliest – men's selves. Self [|] flashes off frame and
    face.
What do then? how meet beauty? [|] Merely meet it; own,
Home at heart, heaven's sweet gift; [|] then leave, let that alone.
Yea, wish that though, wish all, [|] God's better beauty, grace.

God's Grandeur

The world is charged with the grandeur of God.
   It will flame out, like shining from shook foil;
   It gathers to a greatness, like the ooze of oil
Crushed. Why do men then now not reck his rod?
Generations have trod, have trod, have trod;
   And all is seared with trade; bleared, smeared with toil;
   And wears man's smudge and shares man's smell: the soil
Is bare now, nor can foot feel, being shod.

And for all this, nature is never spent;
   There lives the dearest freshness deep down things;
And though the last lights off the black West went
   Oh, morning, at the brown brink eastward, springs –
Because the Holy Ghost over the bent
   World broods with warm breast and with ah! bright wings.

The Sea and the Skylark

On ear and ear two noises too old to end
    Trench – right, the tide that ramps against the shore;
    With a flood or a fall, low lull-off or all roar,
Frequenting there while moon shall wear and wend.

Left hand, off land, I hear the lark ascend,
    His rash-fresh re-winded new-skeinèd score
    In crisps of curl off wild winch whirl, and pour
And pelt music, till none's to spill nor spend.

How these two shame this shallow and frail town!
    How ring right out our sordid turbid time,
Being pure! We, life's pride and cared-for crown,

    Have lost that cheer and charm of earth's past prime:
Our make and making break, are breaking, down
    To man's last dust, drain fast towards man's first slime.

Pied Beauty

Glory be to God for dappled things –
    For skies of couple-colour as a brinded cow;
        For rose-moles all in stipple upon trout that swim;
Fresh-firecoal chestnut-falls; finches' wings;
    Landscape plotted and pieced – fold, fallow, and plough;
        And áll trádes, their gear and tackle and trim.

All things counter, original, spare, strange;
    Whatever is fickle, freckled (who knows how?)
        With swift, slow; sweet, sour; adazzle, dim;
He fathers-forth whose beauty is past change:
                  Praise him.

The Windhover
To Christ our Lord

I caught this morning morning's minion, king-
    dom of daylight's dauphin, dapple-dawn-drawn Falcon, in
      his riding
Of the rolling level underneath him steady air, and striding
High there, how he rung upon the rein of a wimpling wing
In his ecstasy! then off, off forth on swing,
    As a skate's heel sweeps smooth on a bow-bend: the hurl
      and gliding
    Rebuffed the big wind. My heart in hiding
Stirred for a bird, – the achieve of, the mastery of the thing!

Brute beauty and valour and act, oh, air, pride, plume, here
    Buckle! AND the fire that breaks from thee then, a billion
Times told lovelier, more dangerous, O my chevalier!

    No wonder of it: shéer plód makes plough down sillion
Shine, and blue-bleak embers, ah my dear,
    Fall, gall themselves, and gash gold-vermilion.

The Caged Skylark

As a dare-gale skylark scanted in a dull cage
   Man's mounting spirit in his bone-house, mean house, dwells –
   That bird beyond the remembering his free fells,
This in drudgery, day-labouring-out life's age.

Though aloft on turf or perch or poor low stage,
   Both sing sometimes the sweetest, sweetest spells,
   Yet both droop deadly sómetimes in their cells
Or wring their barriers in bursts of fear or rage.

Not that the sweet-fowl, song-fowl, needs no rest –
Why, hear him, hear him babble and drop down to his nest,
   But his own nest, wild nest, no prison.

Man's spirit will be flesh-bound when found at best,
But uncumberèd: meadow-down is not distressed
   For a rainbow footing it nor he for his bónes rísen.

In the Valley of the Elwy

I remember a house where all were good
   To me, God knows, deserving no such thing:
   Comforting smell breathed at very entering,
Fetched fresh, as I suppose, off some sweet wood.

That cordial air made those kind people a hood
   All over, as a bevy of eggs the mothering wing
   Will, or mild nights the new morsels of Spring:
Why, it seemed of course; seemed of right it should.

Lovely the woods, waters, meadows, combes, vales,
All the air things wear that build this world of Wales;
   Only the inmate does not correspond:

God, lover of souls, swaying considerate scales,
Complete thy creature dear O where it fails,
   Being mighty a master, being a father and fond.

The Leaden Echo and the Golden Echo
(Maiden's song from St. Winefred's Well)

How to kéep – is there ány any, is there none such, nowhere
    known some, bow or brooch or braid or brace, láce, latch
    or catch or key to keep
Back beauty, keep it, beauty, beauty, beauty, . . . from vanishing
    away?
Ó is there no frowning of these wrinkles, rankèd wrinkles
    deep,
Dówn? no waving off of these most mournful messengers, still
    messengers, sad and stealing messengers of grey? –
No there's none, there 's none, O no there's none,
Nor can you long be, what you now are, called fair,
Do what you may do, what, do what you may,
And wisdom is early to despair:
Be beginning; since, no, nothing can be done
To keep at bay
Age and age's evils, hoar hair,
Ruck and wrinkle, drooping, dying, death's worst, winding
    sheets, tombs and worms and tumbling to decay;
So be beginning, be beginning to despair.
O there's none; no no no there's none:
Be beginning to despair, to despair,
Despair, despair, despair, despair.

            Spare!
There ís one, yes I have one (Hush there!),
Only not within seeing of the sun.
Not within the singeing of the strong sun,
Tall sun's tingeing, or treacherous the tainting of the
    earth's air,
Somewhere elsewhere there is ah well where! one,

Ońe. Yes I cán tell such a key, I dó know such a place,
Where whatever's prizèd and passes of us, everything that's
     fresh and fast flying of us, seems to us sweet of us and
     swiftly away with, done away with, undone,
Undone, done with, soon done with, and yet dearly and
     dangerously sweet
Of us, the wimpled-water-dimpled, not-by-morning-matchèd
     face,
The flower of beauty, fleece of beauty, too too apt to, ah! to fleet,
Never fleets móre, fastened with the tenderest truth
To its own best being and its loveliness of youth: it is an ever-
     lastingness of, O it is an all youth!
Come then, your ways and airs and looks, locks, maidengear,
     gallantry and gaiety and grace,
Winning ways, airs innocent, maiden manners, sweet looks,
     loose locks, long locks, lovelocks, gaygear, going gallant,
     girlgrace –
Resign them, sign them, seal them, send them, motion them
     with breath,
And with sighs soaring, soaring síghs, deliver
Them; beauty-in-the-ghost, deliver it, early now, long before
     death
Give beauty back, beauty, beauty, beauty, back to God,
     beauty's self and beauty's giver.
See; not a hair is, not an eyelash, not the least lash lost; every
     hair
Is, hair of the head, numbered.
Nay, what we had lighthanded left in surly the mere mould
Will have waked and have waxed and have walked with the
     wind what while we slept,
This side, that side hurling a heavyheaded hundredfold
What while we, while we slumbered.
O then, weary then whý should we tread? O why are we so
     haggard at the heart, so care-coiled, care-killed, so fagged,
     so fashed, so cogged, so cumbered,
When the thing we freely fórfeit is kept with fonder a care,

Fonder a care kept than we could have kept it, kept
Far with fonder a care (and we, we should have lost it) finer,
    fonder
A care kept. – Where kept? do but tell us where kept, where. –
Yonder. – What high as that! We follow, now we follow. –
    Yonder, yes yonder, yonder,
Yonder.

The Starlight Night

Look at the stars! look, look up at the skies!
    O look at all the fire-folk sitting in the air!
    The bright boroughs, the circle-citadels there!
Down in dim woods the diamond delves! the elves'-eyes!
The grey lawns cold where gold, where quickgold lies!
    Wind-beat whitebeam! airy abeles set on a flare!
    Flake-doves sent floating forth at a farmyard scare! –
Ah well! it is all a purchase, all is a prize.

Buy then! bid then! – What? – Prayer, patience, alms, vows
Look, look: a May-mess, like on orchard boughs!
    Look! March-bloom, like on mealed-with-yellow sallows!
These are indeed the barn; withindoors house
The shocks. This piece-bright paling shuts the spouse
    Christ home, Christ and his mother and all his hallows.

Spring

Nothing is so beautiful as Spring –
    When weeds, in wheels, shoot long and lovely and lush;
    Thrush's eggs look little low heavens, and thrush
Through the echoing timber does so rinse and wring
The ear, it strikes like lightnings to hear him sing;
    The glassy peartree leaves and blooms, they brush
    The descending blue; that blue is all in a rush
With richness; the racing lambs too have fair their fling.

What is all this juice and all this joy?
    A strain of the earth's sweet being in the beginning
In Eden garden. – Have, get, before it cloy,

    Before it cloud, Christ, lord, and sour with sinning,
Innocent mind and Mayday in girl and boy,
    Most, O maid's child, thy choice and worthy the winning.

Peace

When will you ever, Peace, wild wooddove, shy wings shut,
Your round me roaming end, and under be my boughs?
When, when, Peace, will you, Peace? – I'll not play hypocrite

To own my heart: I yield you do come sometimes; but
That piecemeal peace is poor peace. What pure peace allows
Alarms of wars, the daunting wars, the death of it?

O surely, reaving Peace, my Lord should leave in lieu
Some good! And so he does leave Patience exquisite,
That plumes to Peace thereafter. And when Peace here does
    house
He comes with work to do, he does not come to coo,
                    He comes to brood and sit.

Andromeda

Now Time's Andromeda on this rock rude,
With not her either beauty's equal or
Her injury's, looks off by both horns of shore,
Her flower, her piece of being, doomed dragon food.

Time past she has been attempted and pursued
By many blows and banes; but now hears roar
A wilder beast from West than all were, more
Rife in her wrongs, more lawless, and more lewd.

Her Perseus linger and leave her tó her extremes? –
Pillowy air he treads a time and hangs
His thoughts on her, forsaken that she seems,

All while her patience, morselled into pangs,
Mounts; then to alight disarming, no one dreams,
With Gorgon's gear and barebill/thongs and fangs.

The Silver Jubilee

*To James First Bishop of Shrewsbury on the 25th Year of his
Episcopate July 28, 1876*

Though no high-hung bells or din
Of braggart bugles cry it in –
    What is sound? Nature's round
Makes the Silver Jubilee.

Five and twenty years have run
Since sacred fountains to the sun
    Sprang, that but now were shut,
Showering Silver Jubilee.

Feasts, when we shall fall asleep,
Shrewsbury may see others keep;
    None but you this her true,
This her Silver Jubilee.

Not today we need lament
Your wealth of life is some way spent:
    Toil has shed round your head
Silver but for Jubilee.

Then for her whose velvet vales
Should have pealed with welcome, Wales,
    Let the chime of a rhyme
Utter Silver Jubilee.

Spelt from Sibyl's Leaves

Earnest, earthless, equal, attuneable, ˈ vaulty, voluminous, . . .
   stupendous
Evening strains to be tíme's vást, ˈ womb-of-all, home-of-all,
   hearse-of-all night.
Her fond yellow hornlight wound to the west, ˈ her wild
   hollow hoarlight hung to the height
Waste; her earliest stars, earlstars, ˈ stárs principal,
   overbend us,
Fíre-féaturing heaven. For earth ˈ her being has unbound; her
   dapple is at end, as-
tray or aswarm, all throughther, in throngs; ˈ self ín self
   steepèd and páshed – qúite
Disremembering, dísmémbering ˈ áll now. Heart, you round
   me right
With: Óur évening is over us; óur night ˈ whélms, whélms, ánd
   will end us.
Only the beakleaved boughs dragonish ˈ damask the tool-
   smooth bleak light; black,
Ever so black on it. Óur tale, O óur oracle! ˈ Lét life, wáned, ah
   lét life wind
Off hér once skéined stained véined varíety ˈ upon, áll on twó
   spools; párt, pen, páck
Now her áll in twó flocks, twó folds – black, white; ˈ right,
   wrong; reckon but, reck but, mind
But thése two; wáre of a wórld where bút these ˈ twó tell, each
   off the óther; of a rack
Where, selfwrung, selfstrung, sheathe- and shelterless, ˈ
   thóughts agaínst thoughts ín groans grínd.

45

Morning, Midday, and Evening Sacrifice

The dappled die-away
Cheek and the wimpled lip,
The gold-wisp, the airy-grey
Eye, all in fellowship –
This, all this beauty blooming,
This, all this freshness fuming,
Give God while worth consuming.

Both thought and thew now bolder
And told by Nature: Tower;
Head, heart, hand, heel, and shoulder
That beat and breathe in power –
This pride of prime's enjoyment
Take as for tool, not toy meant
And hold at Christ's employment.

The vault and scope and schooling
And mastery in the mind,
In silk-ash kept from cooling,
And ripest under rind –
What death half lifts the latch of,
What hell hopes soon the snatch of,
Your offering, with despatch, of!

The Bugler's First Communion

A bugler boy from barrack (it is over the hill
There) – boy bugler, born, he tells me, of Irish
        Mother to an English sire (he
Shares their best gifts surely, fall how things will),

This very very day came down to us after a boon he on
My late being there begged of me, overflowing
        Boon in my bestowing,
Came, I say, this day to it – to a First Communion.

Here he knelt then ín regimental red.
Forth Christ from cupboard fetched, how fain I of feet
        To his youngster take his treat!
Low-latched in leaf-light housel his too huge godhead.

There! and your sweetest sendings, ah divine,
By it, heavens, befall him! as a heart Christ's darling, dauntless;
        Tongue true, vaunt- and tauntless;
Breathing bloom of a chastity in mansex fine.

Frowning and forefending angel-warder
Squander the hell-rook ranks sally to molest him;
        March, kind comrade, abreast him;
Dress his days to a dexterous and starlight order.

How it dóes my heart good, visiting at that bleak hill,
When limber liquid youth, that to all I teach
        Yields tender as a pushed peach,
Hies headstrong to its wellbeing of a self-wise self-will!

Then though I should tread tufts of consolation
Dáys áfter, só I in a sort deserve to
        And do serve God to serve to
Just such slips of soldiery Christ's royal ration.

Nothing élse is like it, no, not all so strains
Us: freshyouth fretted in a bloomfall all portending
        That sweet's sweeter ending;
Realm both Christ is heir to and thére réigns.

O now well work that sealing sacred ointment!
O for now charms, arms, what bans off bad
        And locks love ever in a lad!
Let mé though see no more of him, and not disappointment

Those sweet hopes quell whose least me quickenings lift,
In scarlet or somewhere of some day seeing
        That brow and bead of being,
An our day's God's own Galahad. Though this child's drift

Seems by a divíne doom chánnelled, nor do I cry
Disaster there; but may he not rankle and roam
        In backwheels though bound home? –
That left to the Lord of the Eucharist, I here lie by;

Recorded only, I have put my lips on pleas
Would brandle adamantine heaven with ride and jar, did
    Prayer go disregarded:
Forward-like, but however, and like favourable heaven heard
    these.

Inversnaid

This darksome burn, horseback brown,
His rollrock highroad roaring down,
In coop and in comb the fleece of his foam
Flutes and low to the lake falls home.

A windpuff-bonnet of fáwn-fróth
Turns and twindles over the broth
Of a pool so pitchblack, féll-frówning,
It rounds and rounds Despair to drowning.

Degged with dew, dappled with dew
Are the groins of the braes that the brook treads through,
Wiry heathpacks, flitches of fern,
And the beadbonny ash that sits over the burn.

What would the world be, once bereft
Of wet and of wildness? Let them be left,
O let them be left, wildness and wet;
Long live the weeds and the wilderness yet.

Ribblesdale

Earth, sweet Earth, sweet landscape, with leavès throng
And louchèd low grass, heaven that dost appeal
To, with no tongue to plead, no heart to feel;
That canst but only be, but dost that long –

Thou canst but be, but that thou well dost; strong
Thy plea with him who dealt, nay does now deal,
Thy lovely dale down thus and thus bids reel
Thy river, and o'er gives all to rack or wrong.

And what is Earth's eye, tongue, or heart else, where
Else, but in dear and dogged man? – Ah, the heir
To his own selfbent so bound, so tied to his turn,

To thriftless reave both our rich round world bare
And none reck of world after, this bids wear
Earth brows of such care, care and dear concern.

Tom's Garland:
upon the Unemployed

Tom – garlanded with squat and surly steel
Tom; then Tom's fallowbootfellow piles pick
By him and rips out rockfire homeforth – sturdy Dick;
Tom Heart-at-ease, Tom Navvy: he is all for his meal
Sure, 's bed now. Low be it: lustily he his low lot (feel
That ne'er need hunger, Tom; Tom seldom sick,
Seldomer heartsore; that treads through, prickproof, thick
Thousands of thorns, thoughts) swings though. Commonweal
Little Í reck ho! lacklevel in, if all had bread:
What! Country is honour enough in all us – lordly head,
With heaven's lights high hung round, or, mother-ground
That mammocks, mighty foot. But nó way sped,
Nor mind nor mainstrength; gold go garlanded
With, perilous, O nó; nor yet plod safe shod sound;
              Undenizened, beyond bound
Of earth's glory, earth's ease, all; no one, nowhere,
In wide the world's weal; rare gold, bold steel, bare
              In both; care, but share care –
This, by Despair, bred Hangdog dull; by Rage,
Manwolf, worse; and their packs infest the age.

Harry Ploughman

Hard as hurdle arms, with a broth of goldish flue
Breathed round; the rack of ribs; the scooped flank; lank
Rope-over thigh; knee-nave; and barrelled shank –
      Head and foot, shoulder and shank –
By a grey eye's heed steered well, one crew, fall to;
Stand at stress. Each limb's barrowy brawn, his thew
That onewhere curded, onewhere sucked or sank –
      Soared ór sánk –,
Though as a beechbole firm, finds his, as at a rollcall, rank
And features, in flesh, what deed he each must do –
      His sinew-service where do.

He leans to it, Harry bends, look. Back, elbow, and liquid waist
In him, all quail to the wallowing o' the plough. 'S cheek
   crimsons; curls
Wag or crossbridle, in a wind lifted, windlaced –
      See his wind- lilylocks -laced;
Churlsgrace too, child of Amansstrength, how it hangs or hurls
Them – broad in bluff hide his frowning feet lashed! raced
With, along them, cragiron under and cold furls –
      With-a-fountain's shining-shot furls.

(The Soldier)

Yes. Whý do we áll, seeing of a soldier, bless him? bless
Our redcoats, our tars? Both these being, the greater part,
But frail clay, nay but foul clay. Here it is: the heart,
Since, proud, it calls the calling manly, gives a guess
That, hopes that, makesbelieve, the men must be no less;
It fancies, feigns, deems, dears the artist after his art;
And fain will find as sterling all as all is smart,
And scarlet wear the spirit of wár thére express.
Mark Christ our King. He knows war, served this soldiering
     through;
He of all can reeve a rope best. There he bides in bliss
Now, and séeing somewhére some mán do all that man can do,
For love he leans forth, needs his neck must fall on, kiss,
And cry 'O Christ-done deed! So God-made-flesh does too:
Were I come o'er again' cries Christ 'it should be this'.

To R. B.

The fine delight that fathers thought; the strong
Spur, live and lancing like the blowpipe flame,
Breathes once and, quenchèd faster than it came,
Leaves yet the mind a mother of immortal song.

Nine months she then, nay years, nine years she long
Within her wears, bears, cares and combs the same:
The widow of an insight lost she lives, with aim
Now known and hand at work now never wrong.

Sweet fire the sire of muse, my soul needs this;
I want the one rapture of an inspiration.
O then if in my lagging lines you miss

The roll, the rise, the carol, the creation,
My winter world, that scarcely breathes that bliss
Now, yields you, with some sighs, our explanation.

Moonrise

June 19 1876

I awoke in the Midsummer not-to-call night, | in the white
   and the walk of the morning:
The moon, dwindled and thinned to the fringe | of a
   fingernail held to the candle,
Or paring of paradisaïcal fruit, | lovely in waning but
   lustreless,
Stepped from the stool, drew back from the barrow, | of dark
   Maenefa the mountain;
A cusp still clasped him, a fluke yet fanged him, | entangled
   him, not quite utterly.
This was the prized, the desirable sight, | unsought, presented
   so easily,
Parted me leaf and leaf, divided me, | eyelid and eyelid of
   slumber.

The Lantern out of Doors

Sometimes a lantern moves along the night
    That interests our eyes. And who goes there?
    I think; where from and bound, I wonder, where,
With, all down darkness wide, his wading light?

Men go by me whom either beauty bright
    In mould or mind or what not else makes rare:
    They rain against our much-thick and marsh air
Rich beams, till death or distance buys them quite.

Death or distance soon consumes them: wind
    What most I may eye after, be in at the end
I cannot, and out of sight is out of mind.

Christ minds: Christ's interest, what to avow or amend
    There, éyes them, heart wánts, care haúnts, foot fóllows kínd,
Their ránsom, théir rescue, ánd first, fást, last friénd.

(Ashboughs)

Not of all my eyes see, wandering on the world,
Is anything a milk to the mind so, so sighs deep
Poetry tó it, as a tree whose boughs break in the sky.
Say it is áshboughs: whether on a December day and furled
Fast ór they in clammyish lashtender combs creep
Apart wide and new-nestle at heaven most high.

They touch heaven, tabour on it; how their talons sweep
The smouldering enormous winter welkin! May
Mells blue and snowwhite through them, a fringe and fray
Of greenery: it is old earth's groping towards the steep
       Heaven whom she childs us by.

Cheery Beggar

Beyond Mágdalen and by the Bridge, on a place called there
   the Plain,
     In Summer, in a burst of summertime
     Following falls and falls of rain,
When the air was sweet-and-sour of the flown fineflour of
Those goldnails and their gaylinks that hang along a lime;

   .   .   .   .

     The motion of that man's heart is fine
     Whom want could not make píne, píne
That struggling should not sear him, a gift should cheer him
Like that poor pocket of pence, poor pence of mine.

Binsey Poplars

felled 1879

My aspens dear, whose airy cages quelled,
Quelled or quenched in leaves the leaping sun,
All felled, felled, are all felled;
    Of a fresh and following folded rank
           Not spared, not one
           That dandled a sandalled
       Shadow that swam or sank
On meadow and river and wind-wandering
    weed-winding bank.

O if we but knew what we do
        When we delve or hew –
    Hack and rack the growing green!
        Since country is so tender
    To touch, her being só slender,
    That, like this sleek and seeing ball
    But a prick will make no eye at all,
    Where we, even where we mean
        To mend her we end her,
    When we hew or delve:
After-comers cannot guess the beauty been.
  Ten or twelve, only ten or twelve
    Strokes of havoc únselve
      The sweet especial scene,
    Rural scene, a rural scene,
    Sweet especial rural scene.

(Carrion Comfort)

Not, I'll not, carrion comfort, Despair, not feast on thee;
Not untwist – slack they may be – these last strands of man
In me ór, most weary, cry *I can no more.* I can;
Can something, hope, wish day come, not choose not to be.

But ah, but O thou terrible, why wouldst thou rude on me
Thy wring-world right foot rock? lay a lionlimb against me?
    scan
With darksome devouring eyes my bruisèd bones? and fan,
O in turns of tempest, me heaped there; me frantic to avoid
    thee and flee?

Why? That my chaff might fly; my grain lie, sheer and clear.
Nay in all that toil, that coil, since (seems) I kissed the rod,
Hand rather, my heart lo! lapped strength, stole joy, would
    laugh, chéer.
Cheer whom though? The hero whose heaven-handling flung
    me, fóot tród
Me? or me that fought him? O which one? is it each one? That
    night, that year
Of now done darkness I wretch lay wrestling with (my God!)
    my God.

No worst, there is none. Pitched past pitch of grief,
More pangs will, schooled at forepangs, wilder wring.
Comforter, where, where is your comforting?
Mary, mother of us, where is your relief?
My cries heave, herds-long; huddle in a main, a chief-woe,
world-sorrow; on an age-old anvil wince and sing –
Then lull, then leave off. Fury had shrieked 'No lingering!
Let me be fell: force I must be brief'.
O the mind, mind has mountains; cliffs of fall
Frightful, sheer, no-man-fathomed. Hold them cheap
May who ne'er hung there. Nor does long our small
Durance deal with that steep or deep. Here! creep,
Wretch, under a comfort serves in a whirlwind: all
Life death does end and each day dies with sleep.

~

Patience, hard thing! the hard thing but to pray,
But bid for, Patience is! Patience who asks
Wants war, wants wounds; weary his times, his tasks;
To do without, take tosses, and obey.

Rare patience roots in these, and, these away,
Nowhere. Natural heart's ivy, Patience masks
Our ruins of wrecked past purpose. There she basks
Purple eyes and seas of liquid leaves all day.

We hear our hearts grate on themselves: it kills
To bruise them dearer. Yet the rebellious wills
Of us we do bid God bend to him even so.

And where is he who more and more distills
Delicious kindness? – He is patient. Patience fills
His crisp combs, and that comes those ways we know.

That Nature is a Heraclitean Fire and of the comfort of the Resurrection

Cloud-puffball, torn tufts, tossed pillows ꟷ flaunt forth, then chevy
    on an air-built
thoroughfare: heaven-roysterers, in gay-gangs ꟷ they throng; they
    glitter in marches.
Down roughcast, down dazzling whitewash, ꟷ wherever an elm
    arches,
Shivelights and shadowtackle in long ꟷ lashes lace, lance, and pair.
Delightfully the bright wind boisterous ꟷ ropes, wrestles, beats
    earth bare
Of yestertempest's creases; ꟷ in pool and rutpeel parches
Squandering ooze to squeezed ꟷ dough, crust, dust; stanches,
    starches
Squadroned masks and manmarks ꟷ treadmire toil there
Footfretted in it. Million-fuelèd, ꟷ nature's bonfire burns on.
But quench her bonniest, dearest ꟷ to her, her clearest-selvèd spark
Man, how fast his firedint, ꟷ his mark on mind, is gone!
Both are in an unfathomable, all is in an enormous dark
Drowned. O pity and indig ꟷ nation! Manshape, that shone
Sheer off, disseveral, a star, ꟷ death blots black out; nor mark
            Is any of him at all so stark
But vastness blurs and time ꟷ beats level. Enough! the
    Resurrection,
A heart's-clarion! Away grief's gasping, ꟷ joyless days, dejection.
            Across my foundering deck shone
A beacon, an eternal beam. ꟷ Flesh fade, and mortal trash
Fall to the residuary worm; ꟷ world's wildfire, leave but ash:
            In a flash, at a trumpet crash,
I am all at once what Christ is, ꟷ since he was what I am, and
This Jack, joke, poor potsherd, ꟷ patch, matchwood, immortal
    diamond,
            Is immortal diamond.

∽

Justus quidem tu es, Domine, si disputem tecum; verumtamen justa loquar ad te: Quare via impiorum prosperatur? &c.

Thou art indeed just, Lord, if I contend
With thee; but, sir, so what I plead is just.
Why do sinners' ways prosper? and why must
Disappointment all I endeavour end?

Wert thou my enemy, O thou my friend,
How wouldst thou worse, I wonder, than thou dost
Defeat, thwart me? Oh, the sots and thralls of lust
Do in spare hours more thrive than I that spend,

Sir, life upon thy cause. See, banks and brakes
Now, leavèd how thick! lacèd they are again
With fretty chervil, look, and fresh wind shakes

Them; birds build – but not I build; no, but strain,
Time's eunuch, and not breed one work that wakes.
Mine, O thou lord of life, send my roots rain.